Katie,

MERRY CHRISTMAS ψ

I'm leaving this dedication
a (NICE) dedication fo

Happiest of holidays,
Lots of love,
Katelynx.

GW01072150

The Minister for Poetry Has Decreed
poems by Kevin Higgins

Edited and introduced by Mike Quille

Hungry man, reach for the book: it is a weapon

- Bertolt Brecht

2016

First published 2016
by **Culture Matters**, an imprint of Manifesto Press.

Culture Matters aims to promote progressive arts and other
cultural activities, as part of the cultural struggle for socialism.
See www.culturematters.org.uk

Versions of some of these poems have been previously
published in *Studies In Arts and Humanities Journal, Crannóg
magazine, The Morning Star, The Bogman's Cannon, Facts For
Working People, the website of Irish TD (MP) Clare Daly,
Culture Matters, Rabble.ie, Well Versed, Poethead, & Socialist
Unity.*

Cover image copyright © Martin Rowson, whose support is
gratefully acknowledged.

Print by Evoprint and Design Ltd.

ISBN: 978-1-907464-18-8

Contents

Introduction

I started to write this introduction about how Kevin Higgins's poetry is bitingly satirical, and then stopped. It's true, but it runs the risk of sounding like a cliché, and exactly the kind of cliché that Kevin lampoons with deadly hilarity. So rather than become his next target, allow me to hide behind another, braver critic, who said of his poetry that it is '*a social critique as lithe and imaginative as the con-merchants that run the show*' (Justin Quinn, in The Cambridge Introduction to Modern Irish Poetry, 1800-2000).

The only thing I'd add is that it's a lot more lithe and imaginative than most of his con-merchant targets. See, for example, After The Big Vote Intellectual Begins To Decompose (p. 8), which is a wonderfully savage and vivid exposure of liberal journalists and intellectuals in the British media who after the Brexit vote showed – and continue to show – little respect for democracy. They simply do not understand or care enough about the poor, the sick and the unemployed who have been left behind by capitalist globalisation, and derided by the corporate and political elites that rule us from Westminster and Brussels.

Other good examples are The Ghost of Miniscule John Mann (p. 26) and Coup Plotter's Elegy for Self (p. 45). The ridiculous attempted coup against Jeremy Corbyn by his own colleagues, which backfired spectacularly leaving Corbyn and the socialist left wing of the Labour Party a lot stronger than they were before, was a gift to Kevin Higgins. It stimulated some of the funniest, most skilful and striking political poems that have been written in recent years, and it brought out his gift for cultural ventriloquism, for exquisitely cutting ironic formulations which are as funny as they are true.

These are much more than 'shouty poems' as Higgins calls them. It is political poetry of the highest order, telling truth to power, savagely denouncing it, and poking fun at it, all at the same time. Higgins artistically deploys a profoundly moral sense of justice and truth to expose lies, evasions, greed and sheer stupidity. What better proof of the effectiveness of his poetry could there be, than his suspension by Labour Party officials for writing satirical poetry?

The Swiftian political wit and poetic skill of Kevin Higgins is surely more cause for celebration than sanction. Which is why I am willing to run the risk of writing one last, truthful cliché: **Culture Matters** is extremely proud to publish this pamphlet, and we hope you enjoy reading the poems.

Mike Quille
Editor
Culture Matters
Autumn 2016

After The Big Vote
Intellectual Begins To Decompose

You sit minding that cup
as if it contained, post-Brexit,
the last frothy coffee in all of Brighton.
You've the look of
a pretend Elvis Costello,
or the rejected fourth member
of Bananarama.

Your claim to notoriety
that one of the Sex Pistols
once failed to cross the road
to avoid you. Your opinions
what it said in all
yesterday's editorials.

Your new secret hate
the ghastly Adidas tracksuits of Gateshead,
the sweatpants of Merthyr Tydfil,
for daring to go against your wishes.

Your sneer is a threatened Doberman
with the charming personality removed.
Scientists are currently trying
to bottle your lime-green bile
and make it available on the NHS
as a homeopathic remedy for psychotic
former Guardian columnists.

Your words are the gusts that come out
immediately before
a terrible bowel movement.

Even in the face of bitten
finger nails, the broken hinge

on the upstairs window, and my own
sack load of mistakes,

to be you would be
a fate worse than life.

*In this poem the narrator gives thanks that s/he is not one of the
many UK media and arts intellectuals driven slightly bonkers
by the Brexit vote. Victims of this disorder can be seen palely
loitering in the Lanes area of Brighton, trying to look like Elvis
Costello and hoping to bump into Julie Burchill, or at least
someone who once met Julie Burchill.*

Letter to an Imaginary Enemy

after Thomas McGrath

A might-have-been traffic warden or
social welfare inspector fired for
over zealously applying
what he wishes were the rules.
Blessed to him the police dog
with its well trained teeth.
Blessed the law coming down big
on sympathy strikes like a nice black
truncheon. While the world bellyaches
like some teenager; he orders gin and tonic
and bitches about his ex-wife;
then has her around for dinner
and future ammunition.

A man so serious, they're thinking
of building a Cathedral,
or philosophy department,
in his very head. In all likelihood
both. He stalks about the place,
like the proprietor of an unsuccessful
bed and breakfast, who's forever
trying to get the egg
back out of the pan,
and return it to its shell,
which he plans to spend
the weekend retrieving
from what his soon-to-be
second ex-wife calls
the dustbin of terrible ideas.

*This poem is for those - mostly men- who when they have drink
taken like to provoke arguments in which they angrily defend
the status quo.*

The Art of Political Rhetoric

I am glad you asked me that question
(and not the other one). Absolutely.
Under no circumstances,
except those that will definitely arise.
We need to have a conversation;
and offer the public big solutions
to problems they didn't know they had.
We must build an economy based
on real people going
backwards up the escalator
towards a future in which
they can all equally
disbelieve. The inquiry into these
matters must have teeth
or, at least, dentures.
We will make this country a hub
for inward upvestment from
the Apples, the Googles,
the Redtubes. It's a zero-sum
game between Limerick
and Drogheda United in which
neither team will turn up,
if they know what's good for them.
Hardly anyone will die
because of what we propose. We will provide
the twenty first century hospitals
the squeezed muddle have been roaring
and shouting for. We are committed,
absolutely, to exclusivity in the arts.
Ballet dancing for big people. That sort of thing.
We will fill the country
with so many green-house gasses,
it will float off, of its own volition,
into the sky.
I was privileged to attend yesterday
the least important meeting

in the history of the world.
This is not a time for soundbites,
but I can feel
what I sincerely hope
is the hand of posterity
up my derriere
and think it might be stuck there.

*This poem was inspired by the political oratory of some
candidates in the run-up to the 2016 Irish General Election.
Redtube is a pornographic website, of the non-socialist variety,
whose headquarters are not yet in Ireland, but no doubt soon
will be.*

The Minister for Poetry Has Decreed
after Zbigniew Herbert

That during the Centenary celebrations
in memory of our late revolution,
poets in each of the twenty six counties
from Kerry to Louth
will participate in evenings
of moderation during which even
the moderation will be moderate in the extreme.
Participants will arrive dressed
in their Confirmation suits, or the kind of blazer
one might wear to the funeral
of a much indulged uncle,
when hoping for a mention in the Will.
For poets of the female persuasion
Irish tweed trouser suits
will be provided. Nothing will be said
with which anyone could disagree,
or agree with too vehemently.
Everyone will stand around pretending
to be Seamus, with the best bits
subtracted. The poems we require
are those that instead of embracing
the reader too intimately –
the way couples who've just met each other
at bus-stops in Eyre Square sometimes do –
shake your hand limply,
as if about to be interviewed for a position
as an administrative assistant in an office
which specialises in shredding documents
for abattoirs all over the Midlands.
The Minister for Poetry has decreed.

*This poem was inspired by the fear of some Irish arts
administrators that, during the celebrations of the centenary of
the Easter Rising, someone might write a poem that actually
said something.*

Against Correctness

In the old days, if a woman casually
suggested of a morning on BBC Radio Four
that the old Queen Mum – Gawd
bless her and all who sailed in her – be taken
to a location on the Scottish Highlands,
and made to lie back in a bath of sulphuric acid,
no one was in the least bit offended.

Back then, flaming transsexuals
in rocket fuelled hot pants
could flamenco dance
what they claimed were the bones
of Sir Edward Carson up and down
the Newtownards Road,
and receive only
wild applause.

Pranking students could happily
interrupt the Angelus on
Raidió Teilifís Éireann
to tell the nation
the Pope should be dragged
to the top of Carrantuohill
so the crows could peck
the flies from his balls, and even
the Bishop of Raphoe
would allow himself
to get the joke.

These days, if anyone so much as dares
bring in a law forcing mosques
to replace the call to prayer
with the music of Kate Bush,
or failing that, Ted Nugent,
the politically correct crowd
start making their fuss.

You can't make a harmless
passing remark:
what a nice gesture it was
for the EU Commission to give
every homeless shelter in Greece
one of those Syrian boat children,
all chubby cheeked and oven ready,
so their drowning wouldn't be
in vain; without someone
somewhere making a big
thing of it on the internet.

And a man can't safely admit
in mixed company
that his favourite hobby, of a night,
is following random women
around dark car parks
to see how they react,
without some feminist calling him
sexist or worse. It has come to that.

*This poem looks back on the good old days, before political
correctness gone mad, when you could gratuitously insult the
Queen Mother on BBC Radio and follow women around car
parks at night and nobody minded.*

Against Plan to Ruin Revolution Day with Strike

for the Luas workers

We're all for workers' rights,
like nothing more
than to browse the better variety
of coffee table book for poignant
photographs: cloth caps and blue overalls
whose existences were
exquisitely terrible, down to the way
typhus so cinematically throttled
their two, three, four, and five
year olds, same day industrial slicers
took their little fingers, or perhaps,
if they were lucky,
a thumb.

Because of those bastard
trade unions, we shall not
see their picturesque likes again.
But what makes our pulsing
haemorrhoids pop is Dublin
tram workers' ongoing plan
to make their customers walk, to disrupt
Revolution Day celebrations
by going on strike for money
they wouldn't know what to do with
if they had it.

The men and women of 1916
didn't go out that day
so that a hundred years later
tourists could be inconvenienced,
and distinguished men in eco-friendly
cashmere sweaters made irritable
in their magnificent armchairs.

When, come that Monday,
the ghosts of Markievicz, Connolly, & Pearse
alight at Heuston Station; they must
be allowed go about the business
of watching us pretend to remember them,
unencumbered by picket lines,
or small people daring
to take their share.

*Here, I bravely take issue with the Dublin tram workers who
threatened to ruin the Easter Rising celebrations on Easter
Monday this year by going on strike. It was said that the strike
inconvenienced many tourists, something those who organised
the armed insurrection in 1916 would never have done.*

Ghost of Health Service Future

Back when we had only
the occasional old five pound note
invested under our long suffering mattresses,
in the golden age of scurvy, typhus, plague
there was always something fatal
to take the frail off our hands
at hardly any expense to anyone,
bar the price of digging the grave.

Now, some scientist comes flapping daily
from the laboratory to declare another bastard
disease sadly no longer incurable.
The long term cost of all this
getting better will be our ruin.

The future we offer you will be short
and affordable.

For starters, every cup of tea will be tested
to ensure it contains appropriate levels
of the deadlier strains of E.coli.
Those suffering from cardiac
arrhythmia or elevated blood pressure
will be taken off all expensive medication,
and shouted at three hours a day
by unemployable sociopaths,
so happy at the hint of a job,
they'll work for nothing.

From his or her fortieth birthday onwards
asthmatics, and those with chronic
bronchitis, sarcoidosis, and cystic fibrosis
will receive no treatment at all,
unless they agree to immediately
take up smoking.

Those with Crohn's disease, IBS,
or colitis will be force fed three loaves
of slightly stale bread
until they stop complaining.

Everyone availing of our public health system
will be subject to random spot checks
on their way to work, to make sure
they've gobbled their daily ration
of fat only yoghurt.

Schoolteachers will be empowered
to wire children judged too thin
up to the school sugar pump,
until they have expanded sufficiently.

Those who, despite all this,
insist on turning seventy five
will be tickled to death with feather dusters,
they will be expected to supply themselves;
their laughing corpses dumped
in the nearest river to further
infect the water supply.

Over the next five years,
we will replace the costly chaos
of our hospital system with the eternal calm
of the graveyard.

*In this poem I outline sensible policies for a deadlier Health
Service.*

The Case for The Re-Election of Caligula's Piebald Pony

He's put the I back into Ireland, taken us far
in the right direction;
made this once again a country fit
for Sister Stan to have visions
of equality in. He has worked
with our European partners
to put an end to the centuries young history
of misunderstanding between the peoples
of Burma and Bolivia,
and brokered a Christmas truce
between Loughrea and Portumna
junior hurling teams so,
if it wasn't for the threat of more flooding,
the people of those towns would now
be safely walking the streets,
like they did in his father's time.

Despite the difficulties he's faced,
and those he's not faced,
he's worked all the days and nights it took
to make sure that in our capital city
every child below a certain threshold
has a modest hotel room in which
to grow up and dream
of one day letting in
the goal that finally wins
Mayo the All Ireland, made sure
even the least valuable among us
has a pavement on which to lay
his or her troubled skull.

If re-elected to office, he will personally
give every pensioner
over the age of eighty,
still living in their own home,

a free Brazilian
to help them with the washing up,
or when needs be, the hoovering.

He is committed, or should be,
to providing you the people of this island,
which he understands you call 'Ireland',
with new challenges in the form
of more heart attacks, traffic and pressure
on public transport.

If he could speak,
which we hope he one day will,
he'd ask you – the plain people
of up and down this country – to please
have as much faith in him,
as his investors continue to do.

The Roman Emperor Caligula appointed his horse as Consul.
In this poem I imagine Irish Taoiseach Enda Kenny in the lesser
role of Caligula's piebald pony.

A Day of Just Yes

Word is:

the system of storms
building mid-Atlantic has now
obligingly cancelled itself out;

all remaining car accidents
have been put off until tomorrow;

no further bankruptcy notices
will come into existence
until at least Monday,
as there's no one home
to open the envelopes;

the shadow on your mother's
right lung will not be detectable
on an x-ray until next Wednesday
week at the earliest;

elected representatives
are permitted, for one day only,
to walk the streets openly
shaking peoples' hands
without anyone wanting
to lock them in the boot
of an ancient Ford Escort
to think about what they've done
and what they've failed to do;

commentators from across
the ideological spectrum agree,
even Auntie Bridie's sciatica
is better than it was
this time last week;

the other side's slogans are,
this morning, flags
madly cheering
your victory;

the roof top crows for once
maintain a dignified silence
and appear to be enjoying
this sunshine,
which the old lady in the paper shop
says is promised
to last.

*Written on 23rd May 2015, the day voters in the Republic of
Ireland overwhelmingly vote for same-sex marriage.*

Artists For More Of The Same

#Right2MoreOfTheSame

When the regime begins auctioning
your children off to the Chinese,
and cremating the homeless;
for everyone who goes marching or writes
shouty poems against such things
there are others, like us, who quietly
welcome such reforms.

Our plans have been independently costed
by the Office of Budget Irresponsibility.
All the Artistic Director of the Abbey Theatre's
hairdressing needs will be paid for
by raising the retirement age
for garbage disposal workers
to seventy five.

For their fortieth birthdays, all novelists
of no discernible consequence
will receive a knit-your-own
Martin Amis kit, and the ability
to cause nausea and bloating
in others.

For their fiftieth, members
of the National Academy of Arts and Letters–
and those who consistently liked
the right Facebook posts –
will receive a Jowl Development Grant
(payable annually) and a toothpick
with which to remove
any of the Minister for Culture's pubes
which may have become
lodged between their teeth.

Artists For More Of The Same was set up in opposition to the left wing alliance #Right2Change electoral alliance in the lead in to the 2016 Irish General Election. Its members carry toothpicks everywhere with them, just in case.

The Ghost of Miniscule John Mann

after Bruce Springsteen
"The leadership election should be halted. It is becoming a
farce with long-standing members ... in danger of getting
trumped by people who have opposed the Labour Party and
want to break it up. Some of it is the Militant Tendency types
coming back in."
 - John Mann, Labour MP for Bassetlaw

Men going through lists and scratching lines
through names they know
six months from now will be consigned
by committees of inquiry whose
conclusions were reached
long before they ever met
during big loud speeches
by the late Neil Kinnock. Meetings
held in mortuaries, during which
there was always five minutes
silence in memory of the Right Honourable
Robert Kilroy-Silk.

Stephen Byers MP nailing
to the front of his skull a sign
that screamed 'For Hire',
smoking cigars rolled vigorously
between Rupert Murdoch's thighs.
Welcome to Turquoise Labour.
Traditional values in a modern set-up.
If you give so much as five pence
to the lower orders, make sure
management consultants
in darkest Leatherhead
never find out.

The internet's alive tonight.
Where it's headed, only he knows.
I'm sitting here waiting in the bathroom light
on the ghost of John Mann.

He pulls a rule book
from his NOLS conference bag, lights
up a Benson & Hedges and sets a picture
of Arthur Scargill on fire.
Waiting for when the last shall
live on credit until it runs out, the first
be allowed grow fatter than the bastard child
of Boris Johnson and a blue whale.

Now John said, *"Mom, wherever*
there's a cop beating the wrong guy, I'm there
lending a big, bulbous hand.
Wherever someone's closing a door
on an immigrant family so fast
the youngest child gets her paw caught in it.
Wherever someone's stalking
up and down Ilford High Street
with a placard that shrieks
"Down with Leninist Militants
who wrecked our party!".
Whenever there's someone not scared
to say it's time for good men and women to
poo or remove their posteriors from the pot.
Look in their eyes, Mom,
and you'll see me."

Well the internet's alive tonight
and everybody's kidding themselves
about where this goes.
I'm sitting here in the bathroom light,
with just one remaining flimsy piece
of the cheapest bog roll going
having my head chewed off by
the ghost of miniscule John Mann
here in the bathroom light.

Read up on the history of the National Organisation of Labour
Students during the period 1975-85 and then gently gouge your
eyes out.

Inheritor

for Laura Kuenssberg, BBC political editor

Civilisation sometimes means
rubbing hot peppers in the murderous
eyeballs of teenage internees, or
regretfully introducing their bare backs
to whips embedded with bits of iron.

A chap aiming his rifle
at unarmed Punjabees
until the ammunition runs out
is understandable in the context
of it having been a Saturday.
Those women and small ones
who drowned hiding down a well
would've eventually died anyway.

Sometimes a fellow,
during the course of one
excellent lunch, has to partition
India. You cannot know
what that's like until such responsibility
has been laid out on the table in front of you.

In the opinion of many,
giving handouts to the starving
would've made the potato famine
worse, made them come back
asking for more.

When no alternative presents itself,
making detainees sit naked on a metal pole
is understandable in the context
of it being then and them being brown.

When thoughts such as these
take root and royally flower,

words will wing out of her mouth –
chattering parakeets disguised as exquisite owls –

she will tell you, and you will know,
why those born to rule must do
what rulers must.

Laura Kuenssberg's great uncle was the last British Colonial Governor of Nigeria.

Official Radio One

That time of the week
when bachelor farmers decide,
on balance, not to string themselves
up in the outhouse, bravely
switch on the wireless instead;

on Official Radio Marian the defunct
feminist-to-a-moderate-extent
has a few old pals around
for two thrilling hours
of cream tea and general
consensus. Last month
one critic unfairly hissed

that the show increasingly sounds
like the occupants of a mortuary
in one of the more horrible parts
of Donnybrook, each in turn
rising up in ecstasy to second
what the last speaker said.

Today the no longer discredited ex-Minister for Fish
rushes to agree with thoughts the deceased
Professor of Social Work borrowed
from Conor Cruise O'Brien's
Old English Sheepdog.

A former environmentalist called Tarquin,
with a new special interest in
ecologically unsustainable coffins, mutters
in violent acquiescence with everything said

by the old dear you'd thought long
cremated – her accent still rich with Rathgar -
who these days, it turns out, mostly gets flown
around Africa asking people of the browner variety

what to do with her vast
and flatulent concern for their plight.

*The Marian Finucane radio show on RTE Radio is where
people who still take Bob Geldof seriously gather every
Saturday and Sunday mornings to agree with each other about
the dangers of Sinn Féin and the need for Jeremy Corbyn to
resign, stuff like that.*

The Head of Rabbi Baroness Julia Neuberger

*"Some of this [anti-Semitism] existed, probably within Militant,
for those of us old enough to remember all that."*
Rabbi Baroness Julia Neuberger, Newsnight 27-4-16

It's talked its way in and out
of so many TV studios, people have long since suspected
it's battery operated, but no one can find the off switch.

It's here tonight to tell us
that those who marched that lost Sunday against
the swastikas daubed on Hebrew headstones at Edmonton
were secretly in league with Adolf Hitler.

Her head showed its solidarity more subtly
by spending the day the traditional way,
having its hair reconfigured at one
of the most progressive salons in London.

It's one part Polly Honeybee of The Guardian,
two parts retired Archbishop of Canterbury.

It's spent so long inhaling
the emissions of Earls and Dukes,
it can no longer distinguish
down from up, in from out;
problematic when giving its congregation
advice on family planning.

It's living proof government must act now
and build a secure facility to detain former
Liberal Democrat members
of the House of Lords.

It wouldn't know an anti-Semite
from a Sumo wrestler, and finds
it saves time to presume
anyone who disagrees with it
is most probably both.

The author of this poem, then a member of Militant, was involve
in organising a demonstration on Sunday, June 3rd 1990 & a
subsequent public meeting to protest against the daubing of
swastikas on headstones at the Edmonton Federation Jewish
Cemetery in North London. Rabbi Baroness Julia Neuberger
did not turn up.

What I Told the Psychiatrist
after Woody Allen & Julie Burchill

The cat pads downstairs and its claws
take their hate out on me because
he's been up there re-reading his copy
of The Protocols of the Elders of Zion,
which, one of these days, I'll find
if it kills me, which I expect it will.

Then the wife joins in with an unprovoked
"Are you really wearing that?"
against one of my more
avant-garde jumpers, and I realise
it's a symptom of her
longstanding admiration for
the architecture of Albert Speer.

And there's the shop assistant who
by her very body language accuses
me of being a veteran
of Yom Kippur and member
of Israel Military Intelligence,
each time she rings up my
Vichy bottled water.

And those who've previously
marched and written against
anti-Semitism but now give
tacit endorsement to the policies
of the General Government of Poland
(nineteen thirty nine to forty five)
by disagreeing with me
about the price of parsnips,
or deciding to support
Leicester City. Worst of all is when

bank holiday weekend traffic
gets suddenly constipated, and some
random driver takes his pain out on me
by mouthing horrible words
through his windscreen
because he knows I'm Jewish

even though no one in my family
ever previously was.

*This poem is specially dedicated to the Jewish parts of Julie
Burchill. My cat has since been suspended from the Labour
Party for suspected anti-Semitism.*

The Unquiet Death of Decency
In Memoriam Nick Cohen & David Aaronivitch

The usual apprenticeship:
a youth divided betwixt
bad folksongs
horribly performed,
and being against
nuking Kazakhstan,
for which you've spent
thirty years trying to grow
a compensatory dickey-bow.

For old time's sake you
express your disgust
at how the government's
phasing out the poor –
every day a few less –

by thrice a week feeding
yourself a whole
roast piglet, and reminding
acquaintances, who are
anyone's for a fat glass of sherry,

that a decent leftist
is a one-time social secretary of
Hampstead Youth Communist League
mugged by the Collected Works
of Edmund Burke,
while inhaling butyl nitrate
in a squat near
Hackney Wick.

Your column in The Stinker
a weekly gust
of foul smelling wind
up all the right noses;

if only they'd wake up and sniff
the threat. One of these days!

You kneel
by your bed and pray
to a statue
of Jihad John carved
in a bar of black carbolic;

that he may send
a representative soon
to extinguish Prince Philip,
or blow up Wembley Stadium,

so you can get
back to the serious business
of saying the wildest possible yes
to bombing wherever's next.

*Observer journalist Nick Cohen was a fan of Kevin Higgins'
poetry, describing his 'The Eternal Peace Activist' as "a poem
for our times". He is less of a fan now. Nevertheless, it's
believed Cohen and Times journalist David Aaronovitch both
recite this poem aloud last thing every night.*

Exit

There will be no more thunderstorms
sent across the Channel by the French,
no acid rain floating in from Belgium.
Pizza Hut will offer a choice of
Yorkshire Pudding or Yorkshire Pudding.

You'll spend the next twenty seven bank holidays
dismantling everything you ever bought from IKEA.
The electric shower your plumber,
Pavel, put in last week will be taken out
and you'll be given the number of a bloke
who's pure Billericay. Those used to caviar
will have jellied eels forced
down their magnificent throats.
Every fish and chip shop
on the Costa del Sol will in time
be relocated to Ramsgate or Carlisle.

All paving stones laid by the Irish
will be torn up to make work
for blokes who've been on the sick
since nineteen seventy six.
Those alleged to be involved in secretly
making spaghetti bolognaise
will be arrested and held
in a detention centre near Dover. Sausage dogs
will be put in rubber dinghies
and pointed in the general direction
of the Fatherland. Neatly sliced
French sticks topped with Pâté
will make way for fried bread
lathered with Marmite.

There'll be no more of those new
names for coffee your gran
can't pronounce. The entire royal family

will be shipped back to Bavaria, with the exception
of the Duke of Edinburgh who'll be given
a one way ticket to Athens. Curry
will no longer be compulsory
after every twelfth pint of Stella,
which itself will only be available
by special permission of the Foreign Office.

We'll give India back its tea, sit around increasingly
bellicose campfires in our rusting iron helmets,
our tankards overflowing with traditional Norse mead.

*I wrote this to reassure my good friend Darrell, who was
concerned that Brexit might put a stop to his regular trips to
buy wine in France.*

After the Barbecue

People like us,
always been here
and always will,
until we bequeath this land
to the bacteria.
We were fine with
the War of the Spanish Succession,
only thought it not quite long enough.
When the day gets here we'll happily
bless our great-grand-children as they go guffawing
off to the next officially sanctioned
bloodbath of the nations. But have agreed,
by unanimous vote at tonight's meeting,
we must
build a barricade against this.

Those people's demise –
Thomas and Sylvia, their children Jim, aged 5;
Christy, aged 2 and Mary, five-months-old.
Willie Lynch and his partner Tara,
their Kelsey aged 4, Jodie aged 9.
And Jimmy Lynch, 39 –
in the Carrickmines
barbecue is a tragedy

made all the worse by how
it contented itself
with half-measures.
We won't have the gypsy leftovers put
in the field across from us,
to mar our hard earned view
of the surrounding countryside.

We are not the Ku Klux Klan,
in fact are profoundly jealous
of their much better outfits

and all the great movies
they, without fail, get to turn up in.
We but dream of riding horses
sharp as theirs, as we make our stand
in defence of what we see out the window
when we alight of a morning
on our genetically superior
polished, wooden floors.

These people's Kentucky Fried
relatives are not our issue to solve.
We have scribbled our names
in their book of condolences.
but you, me, and The Evening Herald know
we are what most of the country thinks
when it draws its floral curtains,
shuts its eyelids and tells itself
truths it will never utter in polite company,
or in front of nuns who do great work
in the third world and other parts
of Africa. We realise
we'll be vilified by people
the majority of whom wouldn't have them either.

We just don't want them here,
or, if possible, anywhere else.

*This poem is dedicated to the brave few souls who protested
against having a small temporary travellers' halting site
situated in a field across the road from their housing estate,
after a fire in which most of the traveller families in question
were burned alive.*

41

The Little Elections

Unlike all other candidates,
I'm very much in favour of dog shit;
    have it with everything;
am especially fond of the sort produced by
    frightened Rottweilers.
I have the energy, enthusiasm and necessary
    sexual appetite to properly
service the people behind doors
    I'm knocking on locally.
I'm for more traffic jams
    and overweight policemen called
Frank.
    I won't be diverted into talking
about abortion or world war four.
    This is a little election for little people.
I'm against nasal congestion
    and political reform; have lived locally
for the past half hour.

Our eight year old, Cian,
will support whatever football team
    you want him to. I'm against
adverse weather conditions in Salthill;
    okay, in theory, with the continued
existence of black people.
    I've studied transport systems
at Mauthausen, Belzec, Vorkuta; think I know
    how to ensure two Ballybane buses
never again come along at once.

During the local election campaign in Galway in 2014, one commentator said that "if you have no interest in dog shit, then you have no business running in this election".

The Universal Moderate
after Buffy Sainte-Marie

This poem is dedicated to all candidates of the "centre-left"
and "centre-right" in the recent Irish General Election and to
all supporters of Hillary Rodham Clinton

Over wishy-washy tea in the office canteen,
or when you're condemned to sit beside him
at the after party of a funeral,
the unsub speaks his principles
like he's eight foot one;
but is back down to his usual
one foot eight when
the vote on anything's taken.

Though he says so himself,
it took monumental bravery
for a man of his measurements
to come loudly out in favour of
homosexual marriage the day after
it was legalised everywhere.

He's taking at face value what the Director of the CIA
told Congress yesterday. He's arguing in favour
of the First World War. On balance, he's for
his country and China continuing to mutually
pleasure each other; of selling more
helicopters to Saudi Arabia. He's too busy
giving King Leopold of Belgium's efforts
to civilise the Congo another second chance
to indulge your wild theories.

Be it the proposal to limit the right of landowners
to gun down vagrants wandering
onto their property; the suggested legislation
to make mandatory the rescue by their employers
of children wedged up chimneys;

or the phasing out of compulsory
female circumcision; he's in favour of everything
when the circumstances permit
and all bar Sir Rhodes Boyson's corpse concur.

He's the Universal Moderate,
forever holding up the bit between
those who want to slaughter six million
and those who "unrealistically refuse to consider"
killing even one.

In this poem, a re-write of the song 'The Universal Soldier', the author warns his readers about the dangers of political moderation, in all its insidious forms.

Coup Plotter's Elegy for Self: to be read in the voice of Owen Smith MP
after Chidiock Tichborne

I offered them free ice cream
but they would not eat.
I kept pulling the trigger,
but the gun kept jamming and he would not die.
My voice is lost, and I have repeatedly
said nothing in interviews I'll spend
the rest of my days paying people to forget. .

My prime of career was but a rickety bicycle
with two punctures and no saddle.
My victory feast was but a prehistoric sponge cake
and a plastic cup of lemonade gone flat
during the Labour government before last.
My bunch of grapes, fresh from the vine,
was but a bowl of diahorhea.

My left wing rhetoric was but an ill-fitting codpiece.
This disco's over and I have not scored.
My leadership prospects are but a lock-up garage full of
unsaleable t-shirts and ventriloquist's dummies
that look like more authentic versions of me.
I've tried sleep but the dream's always
I've mislaid my boxer shorts
and my tie's on fire.

Chidiock Tichborne was arrested for conspiracy to assassinate Elizabeth 1st. His poem 'Tychbornes Elegie, written with his owne hand in the Tower before his execution' was written on the eve of his execution for treason. Owen Smith unsuccessfully challenged Jeremy Corbyn for the leadership of the British Labour Party during the summer of 2016 and went on to be the answer to a pub quiz question.

Kevin Higgins joined the Militant Tendency in 1982 at the age of 15. He was active in both the Irish and British Labour Parties; was Chairman of Enfield Against The Poll Tax; and was expelled from the British Labour Party in 1991 for membership of Militant and for his public support for the campaign of non-payment of the Poll Tax. He left Militant in 1994 and began writing poetry in 1995, in an effort to get away from politics.

Twenty years later he can safely say that his efforts to get away from politics have been a great failure. But he's not sorry about that. He now earns his living teaching poetry and creative writing in Galway, on the west coast of Ireland. He co-organises, with his wife Susan Millar DuMars, Over The Edge literary events, Ireland's leading literary reading series.